LM 1063898 9
L
D0589077

THE BOOK OF BLOOD

BY THE SAME AUTHOR

Close Relatives
The Handless Maiden

THE BOOK OF BLOOD

Vicki Feaver

CAPE POETRY

Published by Jonathan Cape 2006

2 4 6 8 10 9 7 5 3

First published in Great Britain in 2006 by
Jonathan Cape
Random House, 20 Vauxhall Bridge Road, London SW1V 2SA

Random House Australia (Pty) Limited
20 Alfred Street, Milsons Point, Sydney,
New South Wales 2061, Australia

Random House New Zealand Limited
18 Poland Road, Glenfield,
Auckland 10, New Zealand

Random House South Africa (Pty) Limited
Isle of Houghton, Corner Boundary Road & Carse O'Gowrie,
Houghton 2198, South Africa

The Random House Group Limited Reg. No. 954009
www.randomhouse.co.uk

A CIP catalogue record for this book is
available from the British Library

ISBN 0-224-07684-1

Papers used by Random House are natural,
recyclable products made from wood grown in sustainable forests;
the manufacturing processes conform to the environmental
regulations of the country of origin

Typeset in Bembo by Palimpsest Book Production Limited, Polmont, Stirlingshire
Printed and bound in Great Britain by William Clowes Ltd, Beccles, Suffolk

For Alasdair

The human creature is alone in his carapace. Poetry is a strong way out. The passage out that she blasts is often in splinters, covered with blood . . .

Stevie Smith

CONTENTS

ONCE ANGELS FREELY ROAMED

Once angels freely roamed,
invisible, but known in a wind
breaking open a bolted door or shutter;

or in the fields, wrestling a grown body,
squeezing the breath from its chest;
their voices – a stern roar for the bold

and guilty; or lowered, gentle,
to no more than amaze the innocent
and fearful – not wasted on the air

but poured directly into the ear;
their touch, on the back of hand
or neck, like the brush of soft feathers;

or at the heels, as when our first parents
were scurried from Eden, the bristles
of a powerfully-wielded broom.

Then angels lost their powers
in the world, replaced by effigies
in wood and stone: hanging

in rows on rafters (wings wormed
by flying beetles); or, noses crumbling,
perched on the lids of tombs.

GIRL IN RED

Little Red Riding Hood was my first love, I felt that if I could have married her, I should have known perfect bliss.
Charles Dickens

I was born to a mother in mourning.

The mood in our house was black
as soft tar at the edges of pavements
I stirred with a stick.

Red was my favourite colour:
scarlet, vermilion, ruby.

At school I painted a red girl in a red wood.

'Trees are green,' the teacher said.
So I painted them green
and she said, 'Red and green clash.'

But I wanted them to clash.
I wanted cymbals, trumpets,
all the noises of rowdy colour
to drown the silence of black.

I got my mother to make me a scarlet dress.
(I didn't care that Grandma said
it made me look like a tart.)

I stole a lipstick –
the sizzling vermilion
that made boys and old men look.

I squeezed into ruby high heels
that on hot days filled with blood.

I drank tumblers of pink gin
and told my sister (sent to spy on me)
it was Cherryade.

I dreamed in red: scarlet, vermilion, ruby.

And now I dream in black.

PILLS

He had to hurl her against the bathroom wall
before she'd be silent.
He wanted peace in the house.
He wanted her tame, faithful, grateful,
to eat from his hand the little yellow pills
that turned everything grey as a sea fret:
butter, strings of marmalade, crumbs
crusted round the children's mouths
like grey sand.
Take three tablets
three times a day. She'd push them up
with her tongue between teeth and cheek,
spitting them into the sink.
After a few days,
when the mist rolled back, she'd strain her neck
craning to comprehend the blue space
birds moved in, filled
with twitterings and cries.
She'd kneel on the lawn,
skirt soaked, rediscovering
the shades of grass: each blade –
like the seconds lost –
separate, sharp, drawing blood
from her thumb. She'd gaze at oranges
as people gaze at statues of Christ
on the Cross: the brilliant rinds –
packed with juice, flesh, pips –
exploding like grenades,
like brains, like trapped gases
at the surface of the sun.

SLOES

He was in Paris for the weekend:
on his own – she was mad
to think otherwise.

She took the children
on an expedition with friends
to pick sloes – small bitter plums
from the spiky twigs
of the blackthorn; best picked
after the first frosts
have loosened the stones.

Her friends were going to soak them in gin
ready for Christmas.

She couldn't think that far.
She couldn't even think
as far as next weekend;
or the stallion, black as a sloe,
galloping above her
down a sloping field.

THE GIFT

You see her in the street
and pull a gun out of your handbag.

That's in a dream.

Awake, you're Medea: imagining
your husband's Greek princess
unwrapping your gift
of a wedding dress.

She slips it over her head:
twirling in the mirror, pouting,
swinging her hips, pushing out
her breasts.
                    Still happy,
still thinking, *he loves me,*
nothing can ever go wrong;
and loving him more, like meat with salt,
for the wife and children he's left,
she discovers the crown,
its filigree of gold leaves
trembling and tinkling
as she lifts it onto her head.

                    Then an itch
on her shoulder, and her finger
under the strap, scratching,
making it worse; and a prickling
in her hair, as if she's got lice –
but lice with the teeth of bats;
then on belly and buttocks and back
a stinging like rolling in nettles;
and then everywhere the dress

and crown touch, her flesh burning –
so she's twisting and leaping,
the cool girl he prefers
to his fiery wife, dripping
flame and shrieking.

THE BORROWED DOG

Her name was Blaze, for a diamond
of white hair on her chest.
But I called her Goya
after the dog in his painting
with its tawny head appearing
over the edge of a sand hill.

That was Blaze: always nose first
at the edge of a territory
on the look out for anything
breaking into a run. 'Blaze! Blaze!'
I'd shout, stupidly, because she didn't stop
for Blaze, or Goya, but streaked
over the fields like a fox: plunging
into a spate river; disappearing
among reeds in a marsh; returning
when I thought she was lost
to shake herself at my feet,
shower me with muddy drops.

She got to think I was a dog: peeing
on the grass where I peed;
pulling my knickers
out of the laundry basket
and chewing the crotch.

And I got not to mind the stink
of her breath; her tongue licking
my ears and nose and chin;
even to love her yelps
when I came back to the house;
her knocking me to the ground,
gripping my arm with teeth
that could rip to the bone,
not leaving a mark.

THE RED CUPBOARD

after Pierre Bonnard

The woman's cupboard, she's stocked
with jams, jellies, pickled limes

and bottles of blue-skinned plums
that just to look at is to taste

their sweet green flesh. Inset in the wall,
the inside's painted the red of petals –

poppies, geraniums – of dream blood.
When she opens the white door

it's like opening herself.
Among jars of quince and apple,

the red satin dress with a boned bodice
she wore as a girl; and multiplied behind,

down a long corridor of deepening reds,
the woman who each month either swelled

with a child, or felt the little burp
and bubble that began her flow.

And beyond, in black red fields,
her mother, and her grandmother,

and her grandmother's mother –
a queue stretching back, back.

Some days, when she opens the door
to find her riches, her gifts, her sumptuous store,

all that's left
is the thick scent of blood.

THE FATES

after Goya

They work in a gang, floating
above the yellow sands

by a black river: four of them
bigger than the tallest trees,

unkempt, half-undressed,
as if they've spent the night

in the open passing a bottle,
or in fitful, juddering sleep.

One crouches open-kneed
with a bundle of threads.

One brandishes scissors:
blades open, ready to snip.

One holds up a spy-glass
like a punter at the races.

The fourth grips a tiny figure
in her fist, its arms outstretched,

eager to begin on its life.
But the spinner of the threads

is still mulling over her choice:
head wrapped in a black turban,

opaque eyes catching
the greenish glints of the sky.

HER HAIR

When she pulled out her silver hairpins
and the wads of cotton wool
that padded her hair out
to look as if she still had curls,
it fell to her waist
in a thin white wisp.

Soon, she'd say, *I'll have no hair left*
and have to wear a wig.

I'd stroke it very gently
with the ivory brush
she'd used on my hair as a baby.

I'd hear the fire's electric hum
and then the sizzles of falling hairs
turning black and frizzy
on its orange coils,
filling my nose
with the stench of burning.

THE CAMELLIA HOUSE

What passed there, in air
trapped under domes of glass,
and always damper and warmer
than air outside, was repeated
every dry day: the wiping down

of a bench, the unwrapping
of gingerbread, the unstoppering
of a thermos, the pouring
of a steaming stream of coffee,
Grandma blowing waves in her cup.

She'd read aloud from the Deaths
in the *Morning Post*, relishing
details of how people died;
then doze with a page of the paper
over her head, while I peered

into the dark spaces under the iron
lacework of gratings, or played
a game on paving paths
of jumping as far as I could
without landing on a crack.

I was allowed to collect flowers
that had fallen onto the soil.
But they were going brown
at the edges, or were nibbled
by beetles and slugs.

So, once, I picked a flower
from a bush – crimson petals
so intricately folded
it was like a flower made of tissue
dipped in glistening wax.

When I found it later, wrapped
in a handkerchief, squashed
in a pocket of my shorts,
I held it to my mouth,
pretending I'd coughed up blood.

THE TRUNK

Like the girl whose curiosity
unloosed all the world's ills
from a box, I wanted to know

what Grandma kept in her trunk:
under a shawl the colours of flame –
orange, gold, mauve – draped

like a sleeping beast on the top;
the bands of black metal
that held everything in.

So one wet afternoon
she opened it up: pulling out
a fox tippet with dangling claws,

a bead-fringed brocade coat;
a bone teething ring
roughened with bite marks;

then bundles of letters
and photographs – Grandpa
who died of pneumonia

caught at a football match,
Jack in a striped rugby shirt
holding a silver cup – everything

she'd kept to remind her
of what was lost. She was kneeling
on the floor, sniffing, wiping

her eyes on her sleeve,
until there was nothing left
except the long white nightdress

she wanted to be laid out in,
and then mothballs
rolling like peppermints.

GORILLA

He was my first love.
Why else would I cycle, every Saturday,
to the museum in the park?

It wasn't the working model
of a coal mine, or specimen jars
of seasonal wild flowers,

or the families of striped snails
and black and white plaster mice
demonstrating the Laws of Mendel.

I headed straight past the jigsaw-
coated giraffe (its head peering
over the balcony) to a case

stuck away in a gloomy corner;
but not so dark I couldn't see
the glossy pouch of his penis and balls.

He was posed against a backdrop of jungle,
one arm grasping a vine,
standing on two legs like a man.

The boys at the dancing class
(I always got the spotty or fat ones)
gripped me with clammy paws.

His hands were like padded gloves
stitched from smooth black leather.
He could swing me off the floor.

I looked up at his lolling tongue;
at his jaw of ferocious teeth.
I gazed into his yellow eyes:

and he gazed back, as if to say,
if you loved me enough
you could bring me back to life.

BUFO BUFO

Clown's name for the creature
in my cellar. I give him gladly

the one room I don't want –
sodden cardboard, wet dark,

the gluey varnish of slugs.
What he eats: dollops

of glassy, yellow-grey meat,
host to scavenging mites,

the only things down here
to move fast. He creeps

over the floor's uneven brick
as if movement is painful,

or crouches still, under the drip
from a leaking pipe, moist

and glistening, pumping
himself to bursting.

It's spring, when toads smell their way
to water, and the females' spawn

is strung in necklaces of black-eyed beads.
But he's my prisoner – soft, warty stone

who at night swells
to the size of a man.

HORNED POPPY

Frailest of flowers, armoured to survive
at the edge of the sea: leaves
tough as holly, hugging the stem
like spiked cuffs; the buds protected
by a prickly sheath; the petals furled
like yellow parachute silk, opening to expose,
at its radiant heart, the threads
of stamens, pollen's loose dust.
It blooms for at the most an hour;
torn apart by the elements it loves.
And then the pistil grows:
a live bootlace, a fuse
of multiplying cells – reaching out
to feel between the shingle's
sharp-edged flints for a moist bed
to lay its seed; or in my kitchen,
drying in the heat, a long thin hand
summoning a salt gale, a tide to roll in
over the flat land, roaring
through the open door.

POND

Not deep enough for a drowning,
or even a baptism; murky, undredged.
I bring my sorrows and stale bread
to the mounting stone at the edge,
fill my lungs with its dank breath.
I test temperatures and surfaces:
water excited by the couplings
of clouds and willows, torn
by flurries of webbed feet;
the swans' heat as they swoon
on the nest, their close-packed plumage
not immaculate – a model for angels' wings –
but stained yellow at the feathers' tips;
a beak that could poke out an eye
in a fierce caress.

YEWS

Fed on the blood of Vikings,
stained a deep umber red,
trees driven by the passions
of xylem and phloem to break out
of the fastness of wood,
branches twisting into necks,
heads, tusks. Poisoners,
their venom in feathery needles,
in seeds buried in the pulp
of the female's orange berries.

I stand in their smothering tents,
the space where nothing grows,
adjusting to the thin light,
the resinous stillness,
the sleepiness of thinking
this would be the moment
to lie down and die.

GLOW-WORM

Talking about the chemical changes
that make a body in love shine,
or even, for months, immune to illness,
you pick a grub from the lawn
and let it lie on your palm – glowing
like the emerald-burning butt
of a cigarette.

(We still haven't touched,
only lain side by side
the half stories of our half lives.)

You call them lightning bugs
from the way the males gather in clouds
and simultaneously flash.

This is the female, fat from a diet
of liquefied snails, at the stage in her cycle
when she hardly eats; when all her energy's
directed to drawing water and oxygen
to a layer of luciferin.

Wingless, wordless,
in a flagrant and luminous bid
to resist the pull to death, she lifts
her shining green abdomen
to signal *yes yes yes*.

ICE AND COAL

'Ice today!' or 'Coal today!'
your Russian grandfather cried
as he carted ice in summer,
coal in winter, through the streets
of Bridgewater, Connecticut;
half the year wet from humping
dripping ice-blocks, the other half
black with coal dust.

You're growing his red beard.
It travels over my body, tickling
as your grandfather Abraham's beard
tickled Rebecca, the wife
whose passage from Yalta
he saved two years to pay for.

When she died – something gynaecological
that should have been simple –
he cracked like ice under pressure,
like a seam of coal squeezed
under the weight of rock.

As you did, inheriting his melancholy,
his fierceness for life, drinking
until all the bottles were empty,
or you passed out.

Sober now, you press against me
a body that's had to unlearn
the melt and burn
that's in your blood.

HEMINGWAY'S HAT

Wearing a copy of the canvas
leather-peaked cap Hemingway wore
at the Finca Vigia – which your mother gave you
to make you look dashing, nerveless,

and which makes me feel
like a Shakespearean heroine
dressed as and played by a boy –
I wonder what I'd be like as a man:

not just brave but 'needing
to be seen to be brave' like Hem;
or like my father, gentle, nervous,
'not a man', as my mother once shrieked.

She'd wanted a son to replace her brother,
lost in the last months of the war in Burma.
I tried – when I started to bleed,
getting my hair cut short as a boy's.

Then, while you raced stolen cars
for the thrill, I changed myself
into a girl – stilettos, stiff
nylon petticoats, a perm.

You travelled from war to war,
until you came here, where dark butterflies
reconnoitre the lawn, and the cats sleep
in the shade of your chair, and you heard

among oaks and firs and birches
a silence like the silence at Plei Me
when you saw the dead rising
above the field of battle.

In our games of changing hats
we float free like those ghosts:
last night, me riding you,
our shared penis

a glistening pillar
sliding between us; this morning,
you washing me, soaping and rinsing
with a woman's tenderness.

GULL WITH AN EEL

What we saw,
but so quickly hardly saw,

was two cormorants fishing
(sleek bombs of held breath)

and a gull riding the currents,
drifting up,

floating down, wings tipping
to keep its eye fixed;

then a splash in the dyke –
the gull soaring,

cormorants chasing; the gull
with an eel in its beak,

dangling like a length
of black rubber pipe.

Already that morning, something
about the blood coming (the sheet

afterwards printed rust-orange);
something unloosed in us

like elvers that you said don't need
a stream to swim up, slithering

inland over wet grass;
like a black-headed gull,

waiting for, stealing,
swallowing an eel.

SKIN

for Alasdair

You watch me rub Vaseline
into my elbows'
scaly armour.

The skin, you explain,
is of the same embryonic
tissue as the brain:

you read in your patients'
rashes and blushes
an uncensored text.

With you it's your knees:
weeping blisters drying
to a hard red crust.

Another million years
and our soft surfaces
could have toughened

into clattering shells –
we could mate like tortoises,
be impervious to love.

BATS

Only at night, the noisy nursery wakes:
the mothers who've taken over the space
in the roof returning from insect-gathering
flights. I can hear the flutter
as they squeeze in under the eaves,
the twittering, chirruping, squeaking,
of milk-sucking, carnivorous throats.
In the day, you wouldn't know they were there,
except for a smell, made up of bits of smells
I thought I'd forgotten – a hamster cage,
Grandma's fusty feather mattress,
the iron reek of a birth room.
I ought to award them honour.
I could take a broom and sweep
their hanging bodies from the beams.
Once, one flew into our bedroom, spinning
above our heads, wings like the contraptions
Leonardo strapped to the backs of men
pattering against ceiling and walls,
stirring nightmares of claws
in the hair, teeth in the neck.
It settled on top of the wardrobe.
I climbed up, saw, in the half dark,
pointed ears move. It was a baby,
just learnt to fly. I wanted it
to be mine: to feed it like my daughter
feeds my granddaughter on the choicest
delicacies, to go out into the wet fields
and search for beetles and crane-flies
and moths, to make it a doll's
soft cot, to rear it with the man
who pulled a sock over his hand
and gently lifted it up, launching it

through the window, returning to the bed
where care is not for the flesh of our flesh
but flesh itself, hands, tongues, the body's
tenderest morsels, offered from each
to each, shared like food.

GORGE

This is the earth's throat.
When we shout, it shouts back.
It only has to wait to eat:

boys hurling stones
over the precipice, poised
as if a breath

could topple them
into the abyss; a girl
laid fainting on the ledge.

A cyclist passes, wheels
inches from a lip
crumbling like biscuit.

You hug the rock-wall,
grasping at ferns
sprouting wherever water

has trickled into crevices.
I walk behind you, repeating
the psalm: *Thy rod and staff*

comfort me . . . though I walk
through the valley
of the shadow of death . . .

I don't know why we're here:
why we didn't turn back
at the first bend where the path

seemed to travel into air;
why we're honeymooning
in mountains at all;

unless we've slipped
through the crust of the earth
and arrived in a circle of hell

and this is the punishment
for coming to the end of love
and daring to love again:

to walk along a path
cut into soft red rock
high on the wall of a gorge

in a dance where the caller cries
two steps to the left,
a little push.

THE BULL

Last night in my dream
a bull had you cornered
between dry-stone walls,
stamping the ground,
lowering its horns:

a bull like the bulls
at the Show – skin hanging
in folds from massive heads
and shoulders, testicles
like bags of stones.

I pulled off the sweater
I was wearing in bed
that moonlight dyed
bright scarlet and drew him
through fields spiked

with magenta thistles –
bare-breasted like the maidens
who led garlanded bulls
to meadows slippery
with thick black blood.

He slithered behind me
down the steep muddy path
to the river, snorting gouts
of steamy breath; then slipped
into the swirling water –

emerging as a man
in socks and pale shirt,
putting on the doctor's dark suit
that you wear as armour
in the wards of bellowing dreams.

AFTER THE PLAY

All week we picked our way along a riverbank
littered with the skulls and ribcages of sheep
swept away by the winter's spates.

And now, driving back through floods,
up a stream that's broken its banks
and is charging downhill towards us,

I think about drowning: the people in the play
crying in chorus like the doomed left behind
when the ark sailed, *God help us! God help us!*

the widow sitting in a rocking chair, front-stage,
keening *never never never never never never*
until I want to stuff a hanky into her mouth;

then lifting her face to the moon, remembering,
in a theatre that almost stops breathing,
the pleasures of sex with her husband.

By the time we get home, I'm grieving
for the bits of you that water and rocks
would tear apart and composing a litany

of what I'd miss about our lovemaking.
So when we do go to bed, when you visit me
with fingers and tongue and legs and torso

reassembled, I play the wife of a man
who was drowned and mourned,
miraculously returned from the dead.

BUZZARDS

Buzzards, you say, *never attack humans.*
They teach their young to fly;
decorate their nests
with a leafy twig.

With you
they keep at a height: looming
out of the pines – dark shapes
shrieking and mewing.

But something – smell,
or an acute hearing,
picking up my heart's
uneven rhythms, or the shared
ferocity of mothers – draws
the female to me: skimming
my hair like a scythe
swishing through grass.

Holed up in the house
I paint pink walls a cool white,
rip up deep red carpets, find,
slipped behind a cupboard,
a photo of a woman
with fierce jaw and eyes
whose spirit still patrols
her garden: long wings outstretched –
each feather separate
like the teeth of a saw.

THE GUN

Bringing a gun into a house
changes it.

You lay it on the kitchen table,
stretched out like something dead
itself: the grainy polished wood stock
jutting over the edge,
the long metal barrel
casting a grey shadow
on the green-checked cloth.

At first it's just practice:
perforating tins
dangling on orange string
from trees in the garden.
Then a rabbit shot
clean through the head.

Soon the fridge fills with creatures
that have run and flown.
Your hands reek of gun oil
and entrails. You trample
fur and feathers. There's a spring
in your step; your eyes gleam
like when sex was fresh.

A gun brings a house alive.

I join in the cooking: jointing
and slicing, stirring and tasting –
excited as if the King of Death
had arrived to feast, stalking
out of winter woods,
his black mouth
sprouting golden crocuses.

RIDDLE

Without you, I prefer the nights:
the darkness inside me

like the darkness around. All day
I am alone with my emptiness:

a white space, with nothing to feed it
but light and shadow.

My claw feet can't follow you.
I have no voice to call you.

I only know you are near by scents –
orange oil, or lavender – and by a heat

that creeps up my cold skin
and tells me I will feel again

the weight of your body. You have no idea
how wonderful it is to hold you,

to have you lie so still, so happy.
When you move, I hear a whoosh

and you touch me in so many places
I'm trembling and tingling.

It's spoiled by fear of your going.
Sometimes, I pretend I'm a cradle

for you to sleep in – but you always wake;
or a womb – but you still escape,

leaping out and leaving me.
So next time you come, I'll be a coffin

filled with chilling water
in which you will stay for ever.

BLODEUWEDD

You've heard, if not seen me, flying
as the light fades in all the places
they gathered flowers to make me:
pineapple broom from the heath;
creamy umbels of meadowsweet;
pale green blooms of the oak.

They gave me as wife to a man
cursed not to marry a woman of flesh.
His fingers touched me like frost.
I fell for a lover fierce as a bee
seeking me out for what I was:
lips, labia, oozing honey nectar.

We killed my husband together.
No one taught me it was wrong.
I was never suckled at a breast.
I never had baby teeth
to bite a gold cross
that hung from a mother's neck.

I was turned into a bird: noiseless flier
hunting mice, shrews, sparrows . . .
tu-wu-wu-wu-wu . . . tu-wu-wu-wu-wu . . .
They know I'm somewhere but not where.
I catch the slightest rustle,
a loud heartbeat.

You find the remains of my meals:
parcels of bones, feathers, carapaces.
Sometimes, I lunge at your lighted
windows: printing the glass
with breast, talons, outstretched wings,
flower face of a desperate girl.

THE SACRIFICE

(after the drawing 'Two Girls with Billowing Robes and a Bull' by Pietro Testa)

We brought him up from a calf.

We feed him milk
from a silver bowl;
brush his hide
until it shines like moon.

Then, we set off: the bull
running between us, restrained
only by the mesmerizing swirl
of our robes – or love –
his head's turned, eyes
swivelling to keep me
in his sight; our legs locked
like partners in a dance:
hock to thigh, hoof
to bare foot.
When the knife
touches his throat, he swoons
into its edge, blood falling
in bright gobs on earth
where corn will sprout
green and gold.

I walk home, headachey,
a little sick, and rinse my clothes
in a spring that flows, pure
and cold from the hills;
squeezing and gently rubbing
gauzy cloth, the stone basin
filling with rust clouds
and running clear again.

MEDEA'S LITTLE BROTHER

Grab the boy! Jason yelled.
So I scooped him up:
my father's darling
who thought it was a game
of chase.
            At sea
we fed him oranges, sticky treats.
He fell asleep in a nest of ropes.
We watched the empty blanket
of the waves; kissed with mouths
salt with spray.
                        And then a speck
that grew, became a boat:
my purple-robed father
roaring from the prow.

I lifted him, heavy, warm,
still flushed with sleep;
cradled him, crooning,
like when I'd teased a splinter
from his poisoned thumb –
clever big sister who knew the arts
of taking away pain.

Then, I wrenched back his arm.
(It made a little click
like wringing the neck
of a cock.)

I didn't know he was so brave.
I thought he'd scream.
I thought he'd scream
and my father would hear
and drop his boat's sails.

But he put up more sail:
stealing our wind. His boat
was almost on ours: men
with grappling hooks
hanging from the gunnels.

There was a moment of calm:
our boom swung idly;
our mainsheet flapped.
I thought: I'll make a splint
with an oar; we'll sail
for a shore where the trees
have a healing bark.

Then Jason gave me that look:
If you really love me
you'll know what to do.

And I gripped my brother's arm –
twisting and pulling
until the flesh tore
and the bone ripped
out of the socket, hurling it
into our creamy wake.
And then his other arm,
and a leg, and his other leg,
so the water frothed red;
and then his golden-curled head.

HEAT AND COLD

(Keats's House, Piazza de Spagna)

They burned the bedding and furniture;
fumigated with sulphur; repainted
walls, doors, windows; the ceiling's
embossed flowers that made you think
of daisies growing on your grave,
picked out in white and red.

The only thing left you touched
is the fireplace: fingering
its carved garlands; the little lion-
(or is it devil-shaped?) medallions;
pressing your hot forehead
to the cold marble mantle.

Your face rises from the mask
but with the colours of life:
cavernous purple-ringed eyes;
cheeks with the tell-tale bright spots
of the disease in which blood
bubbles from the lungs.

It's winter: ice in the square.
You stand at the window
listening to the fountain: Bernini's
land-locked stone boat, running over
and refilling, hung with icicles
like a ship at the Pole.

Then you hunch, shivering
over burning coals, sipping
a cup of dewy milk (the only thing
you still enjoy the taste of).
Everything's extremes
of heat and cold: the cap

Fanny made that scalds
your scalp; her cornelian egg
(for cooling dressmaker's fingers)
that you pass from hand to hand
like someone getting up courage
to enter a freezing ocean.

THE MAN WHO ATE STONES

He had never felt so light:
his skin like the paper of kites;

his bones like the inside of Maltesers.
He thought he was going to float

through the roof of the house,
drifting through space

like an astronaut
untethered from his craft.

He begged his wife to hold him down
but she just laughed.

So he drove to the beach and knelt
at the edge of the sea,

swallowing pebbles to weight
his stomach with ballast.

The water was black, except where the moon
lit fires in the breaking waves.

He saw the god whose home
is under the ocean's storms:

the bubbles of his breath
shooting to the surface.

Here was another man
who had to eat stones.

He plunged into the burning water
to meet him.

THE WOMAN WHO TALKED TO HER TEETH

She'd had her teeth out in her teens.
Lots of girls did it.
Dentists were expensive:
you got fitted with a false set
before marriage and kids.

What did she want with teeth?
She'd still got a jagged scar
where the neighbour's dog
had bitten her cheek.
She didn't even make bridesmaid.

She kept her lips shut
to hide the hole in her mouth.
She ate the kind of food
that slipped past her gums:
gallons of soup and ice-cream.

They talked her into it for her Sixtieth.
False teeth were different now:
pearly, better than real.
She could have a perm, too.
And a new party dress.

She agreed, wanting the dress.
But the teeth never went into her mouth.
She'd lay them on the grass,
jaws slightly open
so they seemed to be smiling.

Then she'd sit beside them
(at a safe distance,
in case they turned nasty)
and tell them the stories
she would have told her children.

THE CYCLIST

in memoriam

You pull on a yellow vest,
and black shorts with a chamois pad
at the crotch, fill two water bottles
with weak lemon squash, take bacon
and lettuce butties that your mother
left in the fridge; shut the back door,
quietly, so as not to wake her;
then you wheel your bike
from the shed: cleaned, oiled,
and with the gears honed
to a precision worked on for hours.

It's a beautiful day: sun,
hardly a wind, the scent of cut grass
from the verges; violets, primroses,
and red campion on the banks.

On the hills, you pretend
you're winding your way up a rope.
Coming down, you let the bike go –
little pieces of grit flying up
from the wheels.
                    You stop
by the river: splashing icy water
on your face; watching trout
and trout shadows holding still
in the current.
                    Then, you're racing
to make up lost time: blood pumping
from your heart to shoulders, wrists,
thighs, calves; muscles contracting,

relaxing, without interference
from the brain.

                                        If you were thinking
of anything, it's the first gulp of beer
in the pub; licking a moustache
of froth from your top lip;
of tonight, if you're lucky,
slipping hot blistered hands
round the lovely pulpy weight
of a girl's breasts.

SPIDER

You hung above my basin for weeks.
It didn't bother you – the buzzing
my electric toothbrush makes,
or the looming bush of silver hair
as I lowered my head to spit.

You were like a nun
feeding on crumbs of God.
I talked to you, not as to a pet,
but as if your contemplations
had given you a higher wisdom.

Then it got to me: the way
nothing fazed you and that
you didn't deign to talk back –
just dangled like fine fuse wire,
the frame of a ghost tent.

Maybe you were dead?
I poked your thread with my finger.
And now I'm standing on a chair
craning my neck to see
where you've disappeared.

ST AGATHA'S BREASTS

after a painting by Giovanni Busi, born c.1485

I grew up in the shadow
of Marilyn's breasts, sneaking
sideways looks at other girls
in the showers, at bumps
that month after month
swelled like fruits
in a heated greenhouse.

A woman wasn't a woman
without breasts.

Then, one after another, friends
lost their breasts, grieved
and carried on: under blouses
and sweaters the secret
of pink prostheses.

And now, I look at you: saint
whose breasts were cut off with shears.

They're set beside you
in a shallow glass dish
like glazed apples.

You're squeezing one
as a woman might
to express milk,
or excite a gazer's passion.

MY EARS

Peasant's ears, my ex
pronounced them: ears,
(unlike his great-lobed lugs

proclaiming his descent
from bishops and kings)
with almost no lobes:

ears thudding with the blood
of serfs and small farmers,
of vagrants and poachers,

that curl up at the braying
of royals, sleep through
the droning of clerics and,

when insulted, burn red
like Grandma's (who kept bantams
in her backyard in Wigan);

ears turned to babies' cries
and the wild geese's
flying orchestras;

ears that as a child
I pressed to the rumbling sides
of slumbering cows.

LISTENING TO MY HEART

It began faintly – a fluttering
like a butterfly trapped
behind glass; got harder,
sharper – the Morse
of a beak tapping
on the wall of an egg.

On holiday on Hydra,
I watched fishermen
unloading their catch,
tossing heads and guts
to waiting cats; climbed
steep cobbled steps

and had to lean on a wall, staring
at white dust, listening
to a raga of cicadas
and puttering outboards
as the boats headed off
for another harbour.

It happened again, one night
on Worthing station: rain
drumming on the glass roof;
my pulse picking up
the juddering rhythms
of through trains.

Finally, my heart woke me
in my own bed: drowning
the whirling cries of curlews;
pounding like the keys
of an old typewriter
racing to the end of a story.

THE BOOK OF BLOOD

It was discovered in her hotel room,
under a layer of clean underwear
at the bottom of her suitcase:

a ledger with columns labelled
'name', 'age', 'race', 'place', 'date',
and 'manner of killing' (*'fire-bomb*

thrown into cellar', 'beaten
with nail-studded club'); filled in
with sepia ink in a spiky italic script.

Her son flew out to identify her body.
He'd thought she was travelling the world
collecting wild flowers.

He remembered gentians
from the moors above Teesdale
pressed between wads of blotting;

and the book where she'd sellotaped
dried specimens: recording name, date,
and place where they were found.

BIRD WOMAN

There was a bird in her chest.

Its cry flew from her throat –
piercing and mournful
as a peewit's.

She could feel its beak
pecking the soft flesh
of her breasts.

She gathered mimulas from the streams
with little bloodspots
on their yellow lower lips;
and the venous red heads
of spiny marsh thistles;
and stones that she'd split
to find fossils of primitive worms.

She made a tent on the lawn,
draping old velvet curtains
over a wooden clothes' horse;
arranging flowers and stones
like a bowerbird decorating
the tunnel of courtship.

She bought it a china snowy owl
as a mate.

But it was happiest
in the heat and feathery softness
of her bed, dreaming of flying –
wings beating against the cage
of her ribs, or practising its drop
onto a young rabbit or leveret,
claws like a peregrine's
clamped round her heart.

CINDERELLA

I'm an artist of the hearth:
dresses in tatters
from flying sparks;

skin scarred
from falling logs.

I love fire
and the pictures in fire.

But I love dead fire best:

rolling in cinders
until I'm glittery
with flakes of ash;

sticking my head
into the chimney's
black velvet throat.

When I'm dirty enough,
smothered in soot
and fire dust,

I print the shapes of grief

hands
feet
breasts
belly
open mouth

onto fine linen sheets.

THE BLUE BUTTERFLY

It flew out of the corner of a red eye

butterfly
like a cut-out
from Greek sky

flitting
over sphagnum
and heather

diving
into scratchy shoots

then flying off over the machair

opening and closing wings
whose undersides
had the metallic
grey-green sheen
of a plane.

It settled on a head of sheepsbit

flower
like a small round brooch
set with blue stones

the two blues – the heavenly blue
of the butterfly

the smoky blue of earth's
deepest caverns –

meeting in mid-kiss.

NOTES & ACKNOWLEDGEMENTS

The Gift
See Euripides' *Medea* for a fuller account of Medea's revenge on Glauce.

The Red Cupboard
The cupboard in the painting is Bonnard's wife's cupboard. In Homer's *Odyssey* the souls of the dead are desperate to drink blood to revitalise their souls.

The Fates
Las Parcas (*The Fates*), one of Goya's 'Black Paintings', is in The Prado, Madrid. Classical tradition has three fates, represented as old women spinning, who decide the trajectory of a life at birth. Clotho holds the distaff, Lachesis pulls out the thread, and Atropos cuts it short.

Gorilla
The gorilla is still locked in his case in the Natural History Museum at Wollaton Hall, Nottingham. Postcards of him are on sale in the Museum shop.

Horned Poppy
These strange flowers are native to shingle beaches in the South East of England.

Yews
The ancient yews at Kingley Vale, West Sussex, grow on the site of a battle with the Vikings.

Hemingway's Hat
Plei Me was the site of a US Special Forces Camp in the Vietnam War. It was besieged for several days by units from the Viet Cong and North Vietnamese People's Army.

The Sacrifice
The drawing, based on a panel from the Nike frieze, is in the National Gallery of Scotland.

St Agatha's Breasts
The painting of St Agatha is in the National Gallery of Scotland.

Medea's Little Brother
The poem is based on an episode from the Medea legend as told by Rex Warner in *Men and Gods*: 'When the king discovered that his daughter had fled with Jason, he determined to overtake them and sailed in pursuit with his whole fleet. Once more Medea saved her husband and the Greeks, but she only saved them by doing a terrible deed. She had taken with her her little brother Absyrtus. Now she killed the boy and threw on the water pieces of body, so that King Aetes would delay his pursuit in order to collect the fragments of his son's body for burial.'

Blodeuwedd
Blodeuwedd is the Welsh word for owl and means 'flower-face'. The story is from the Mabinogion cycle.

Acknowledgements are due to the editors of the following:

Arvon Anthology, Boomerang, Columbia, Heat, Independent on Sunday, London Review of Books, Magma, Markings, Mslexia, New Yorker, New Writing Scotland, Oxford Magazine, Poetry Review, Smith's Knoll

'Buzzards' was read on *Words on the Street* (BBC Radio 4); 'Bats' won second prize in the National Poetry Competition.

Some of the poems have previously appeared in the following books: *Mind Readings* (Minerva), *The New Exeter Book of Riddles* (Enitharmon), *New Writing 12* (Picador), *Out of Fashion* (Faber), *Penguin Modern Poets 2, Sussex Seams* (Alan Sutton Publishing).

Grateful thanks are due to the Arts Council of England for a 1998 Writers' Award.

I would also like to thank Robin Robertson, my patient and brilliant editor at Cape; Jane Feaver for her astute tweaking and pruning; Jessica Feaver for taming the toad; Matthew Sweeney for bringing order; Alasdair Young for giving flight to some good poems and shooting down some dud ones; also, among others, Andrew Forster, Mario Relich, Elspeth Brown, Norman Kreitman, Stephanie Norgate, Alison MacLeod, Hugh Dunkerley, George Marsh, Génie Turton, and my friends from Dolphinton Writers, Fiona Gibson, Amanda McLean, Pam Taylor, Elizabeth Dobie and Tania Cheston; and finally Dr Joanna Schachter, who is one of the spirits behind this book, and was never properly acknowledged for her support with *The Handless Maiden*.